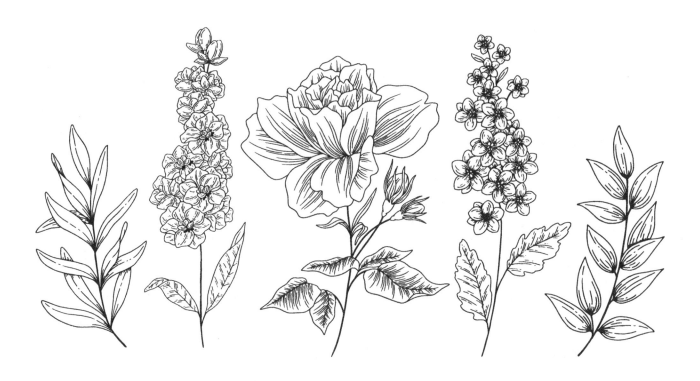

this book belongs to

....

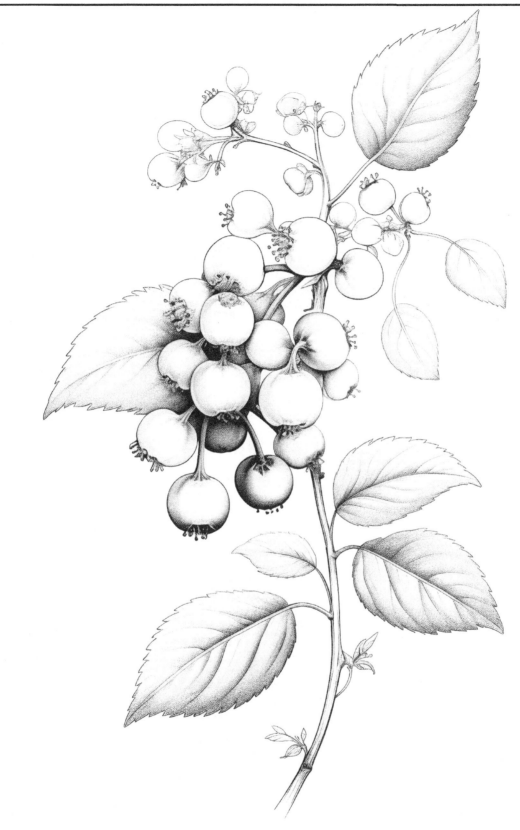

"Realize deeply that the present moment is all you have. Make the now the primary focus of your life."
-Eckhart Tolle

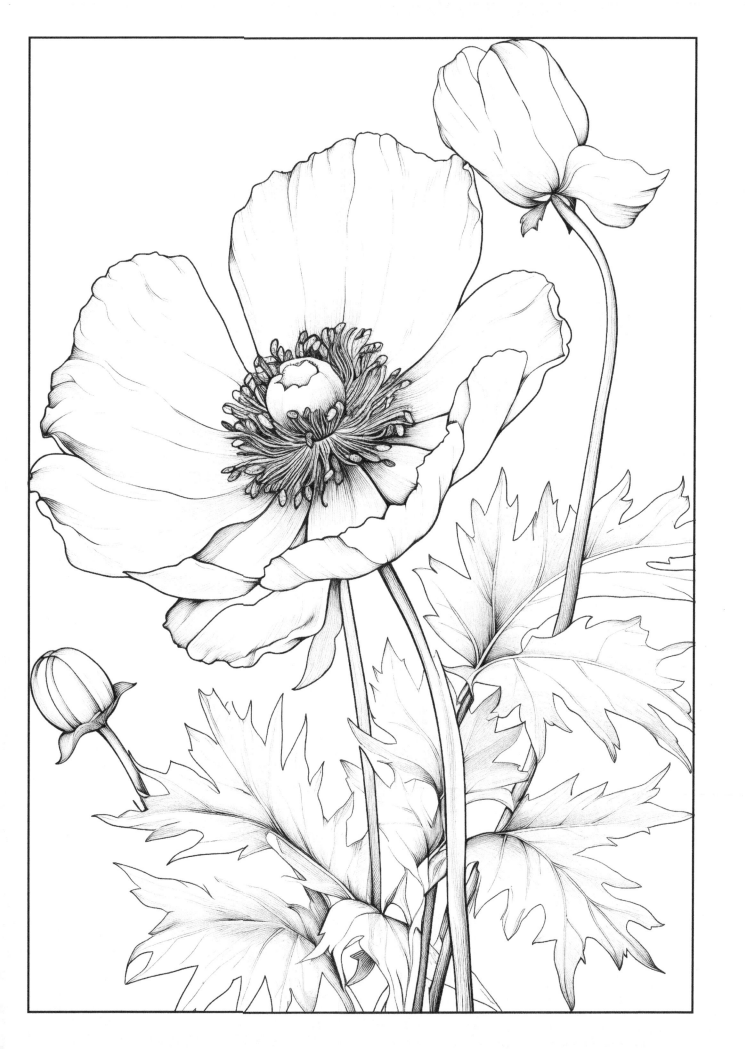

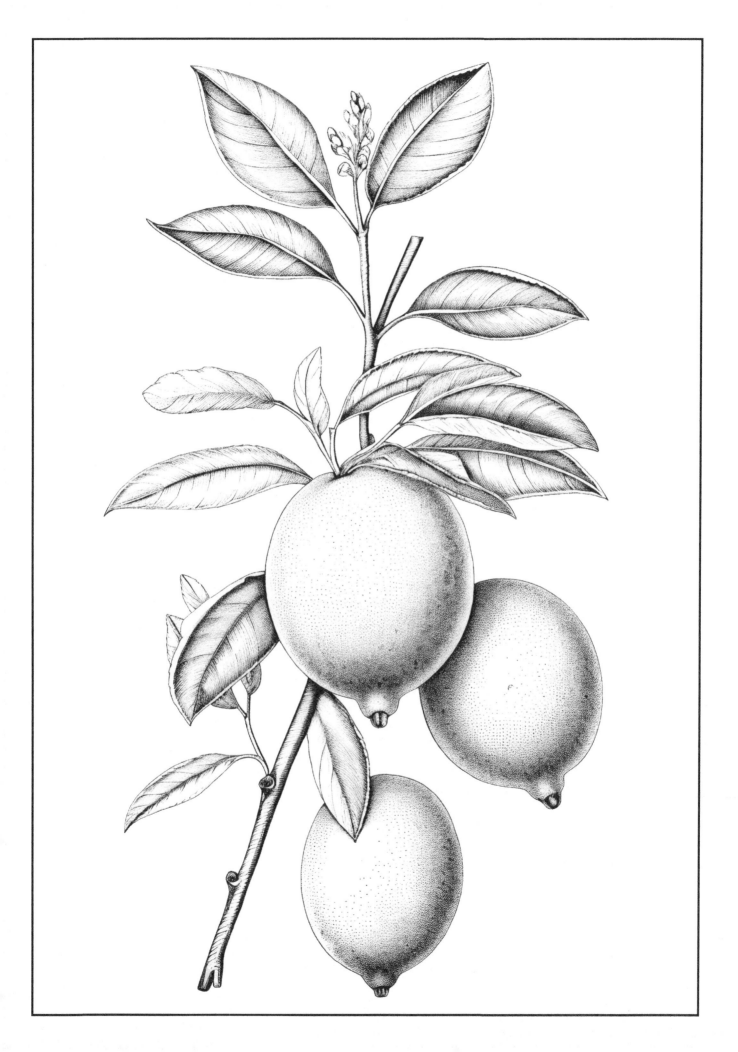

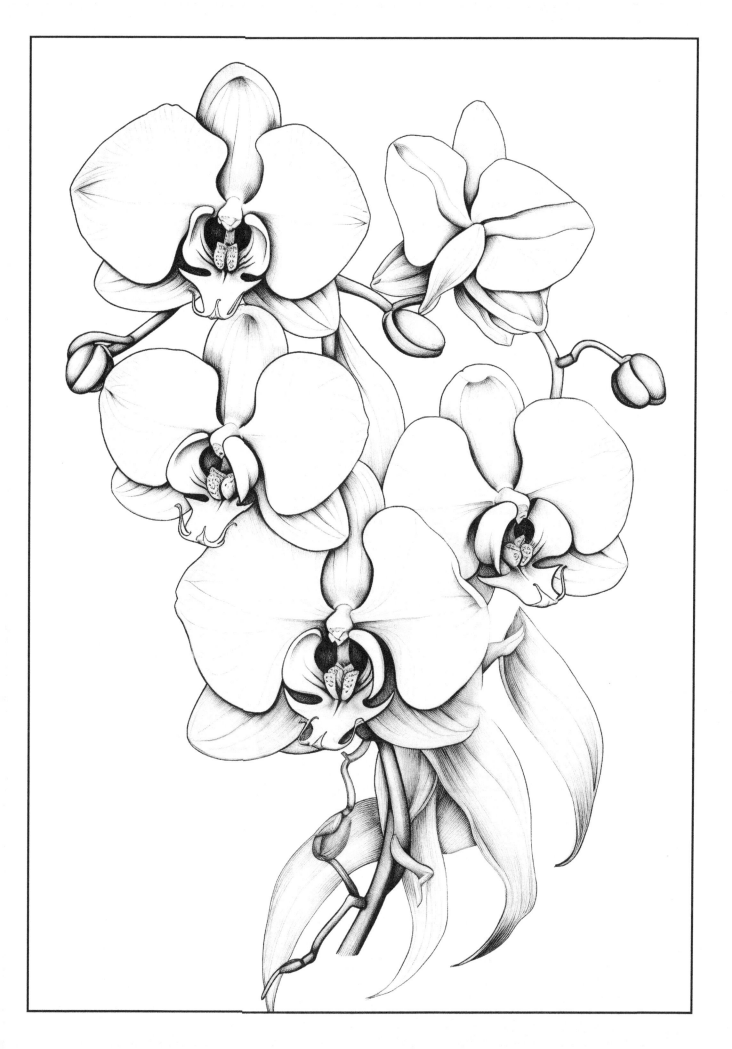

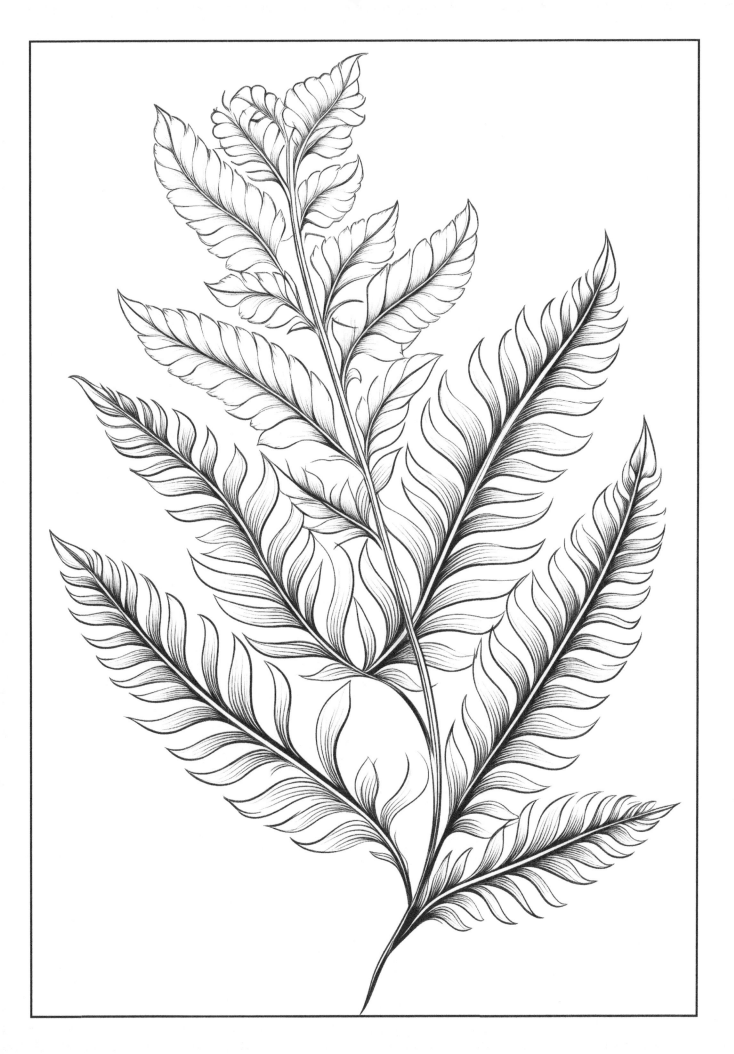

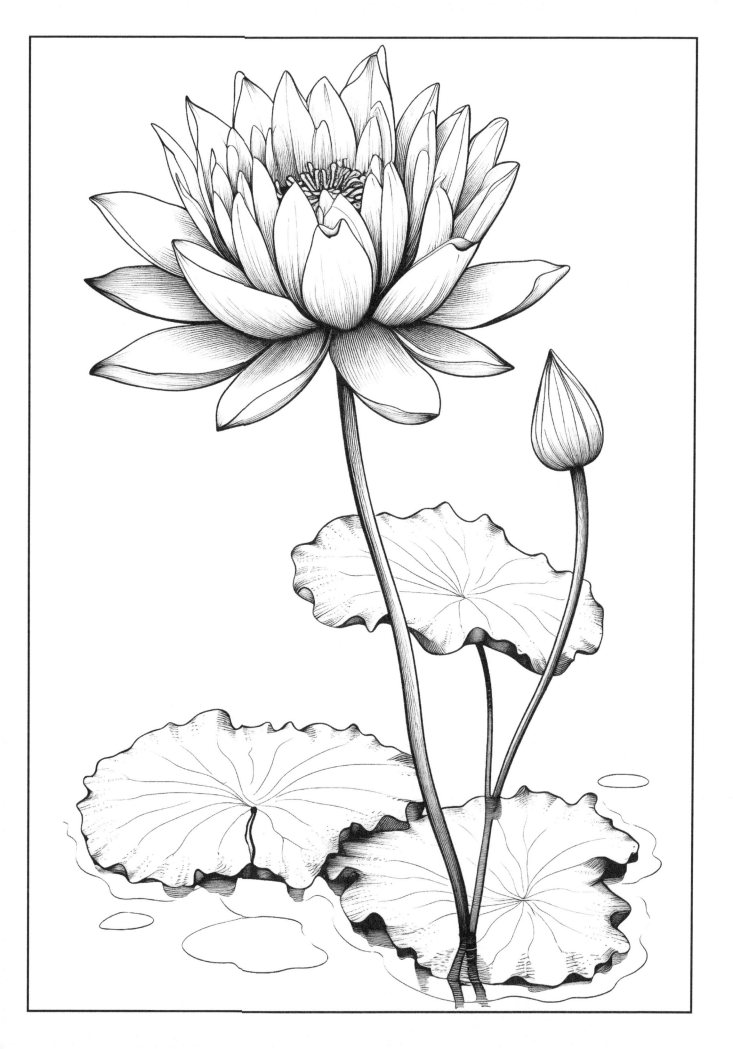

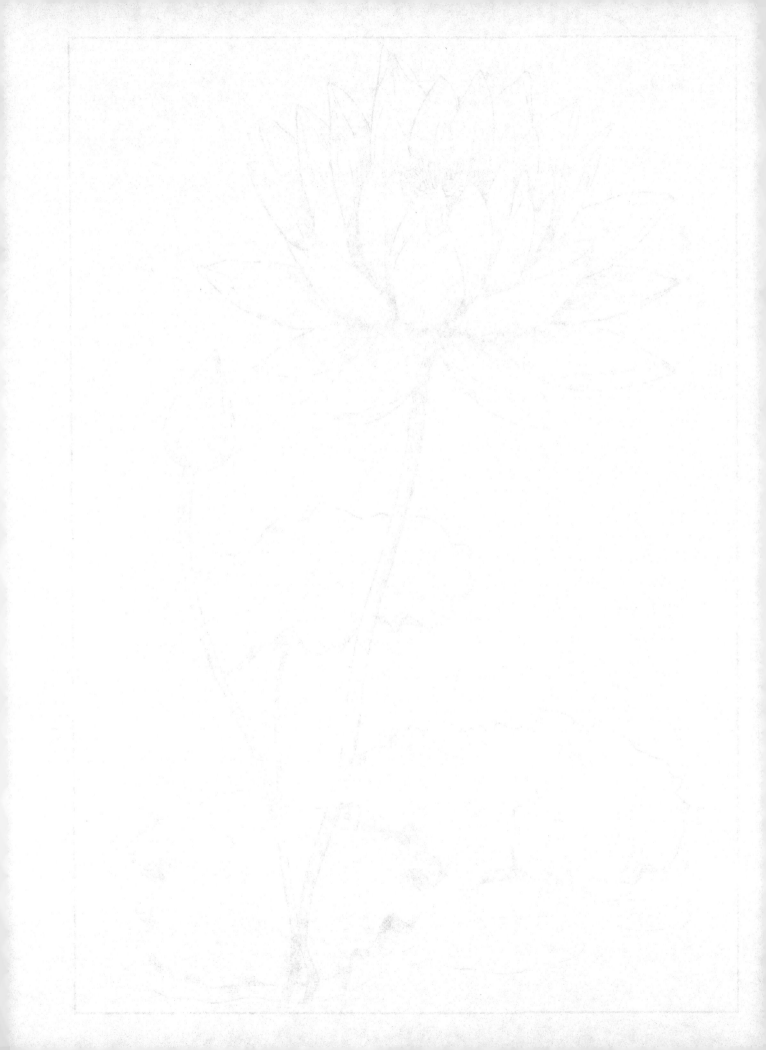

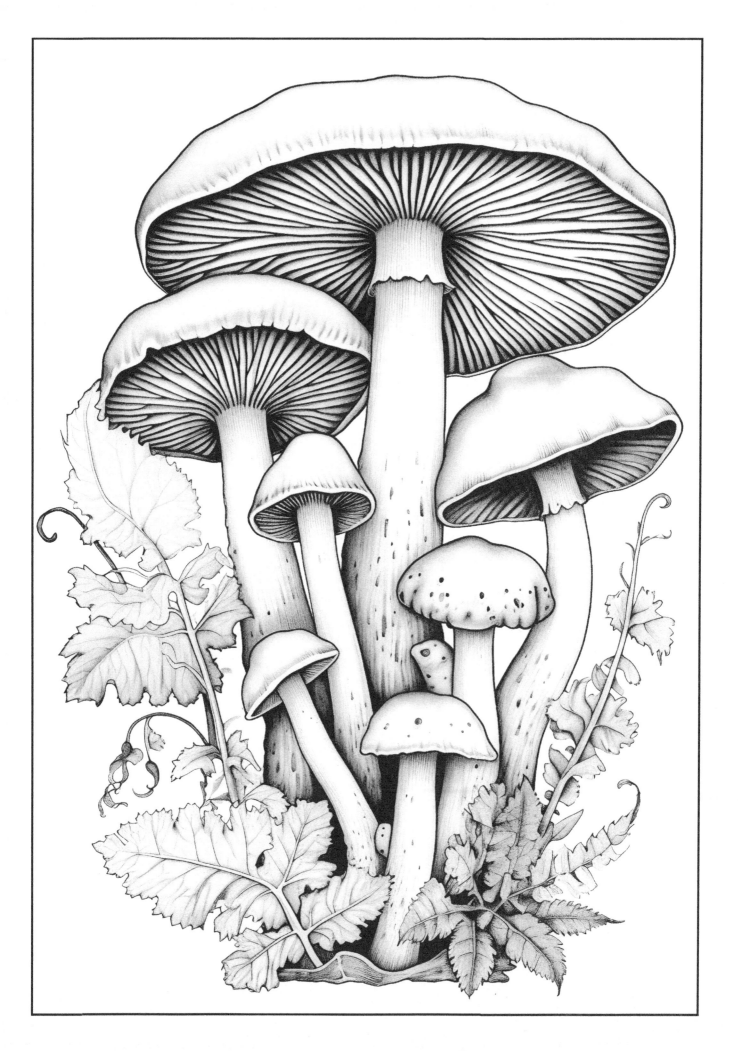

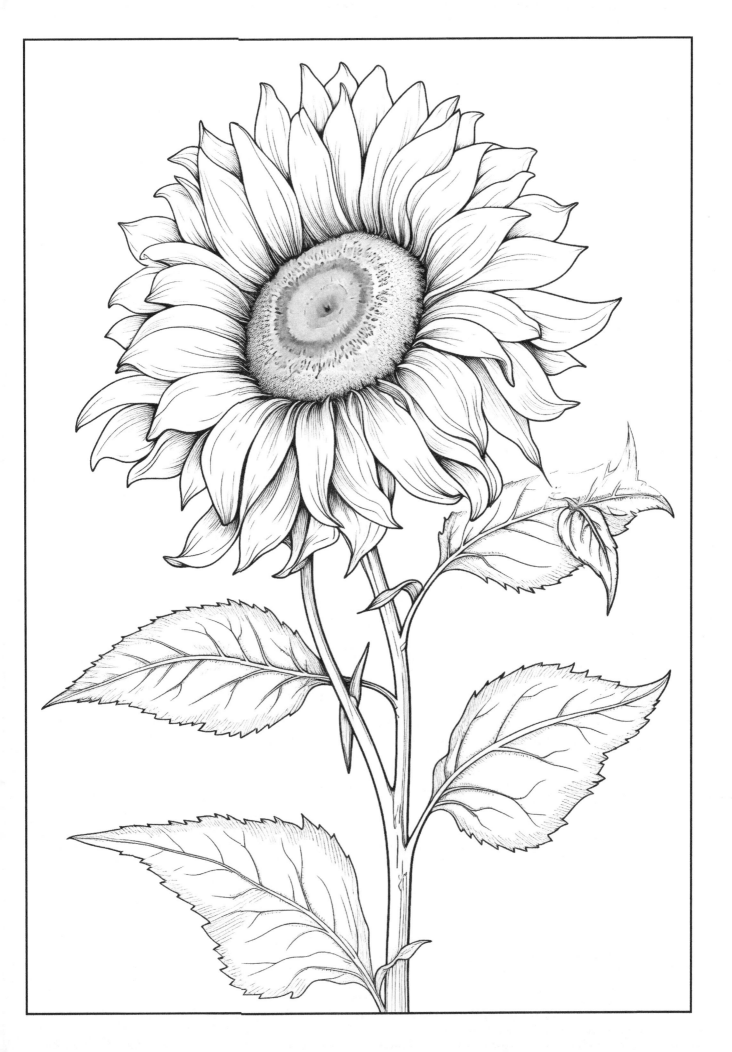

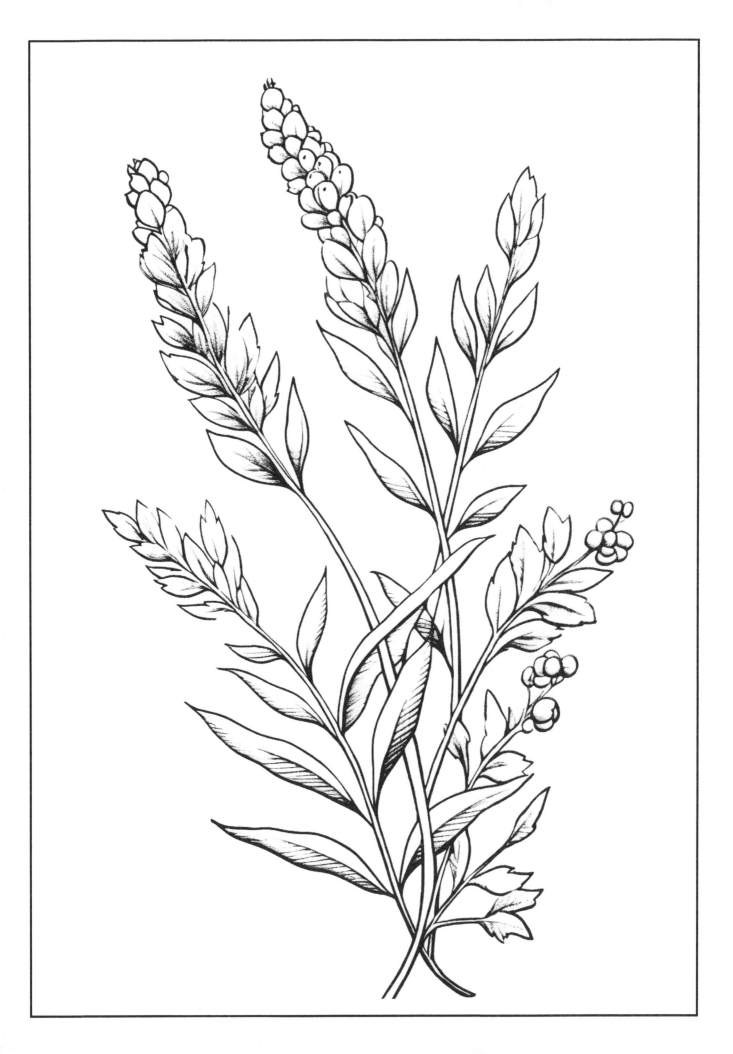

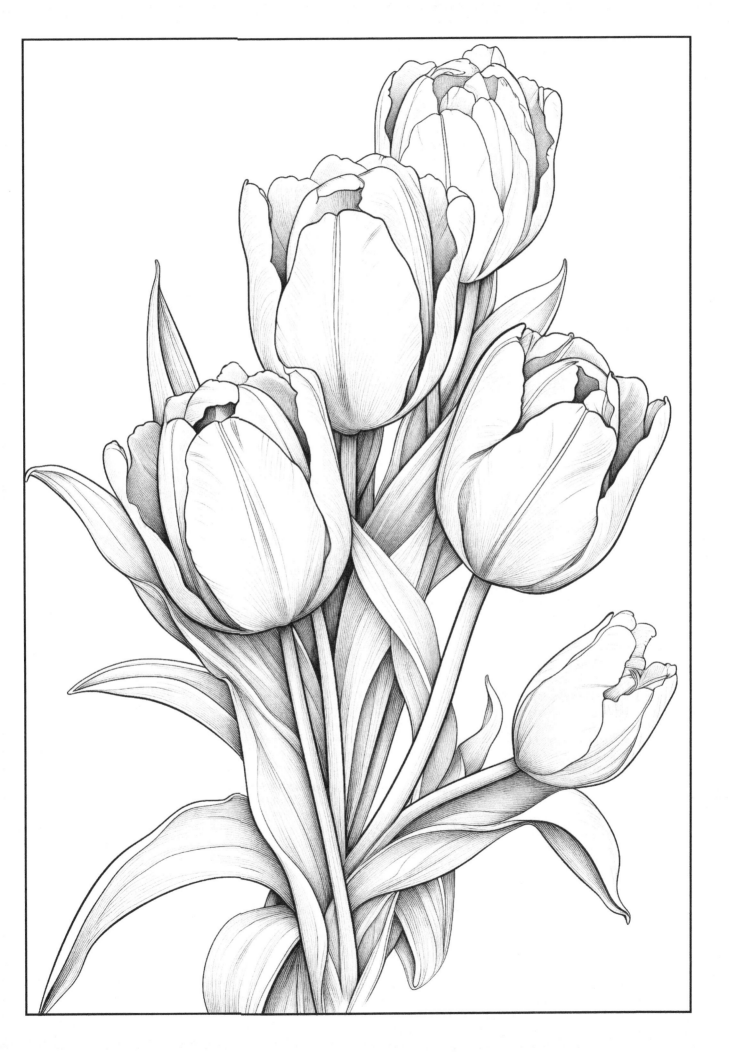

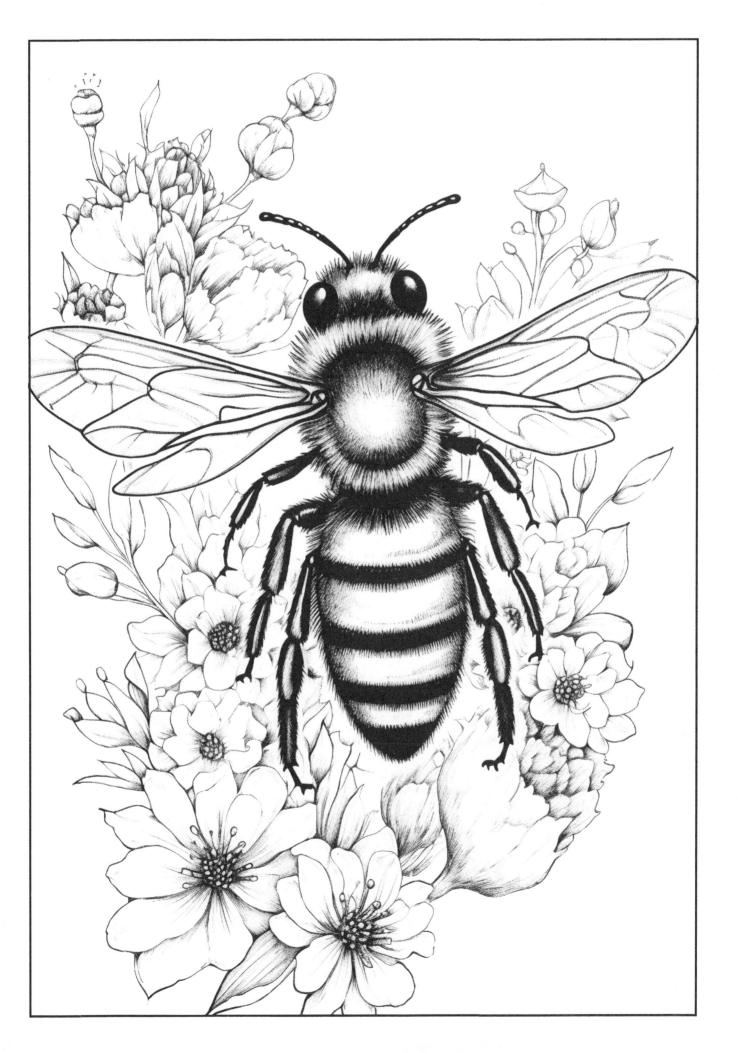

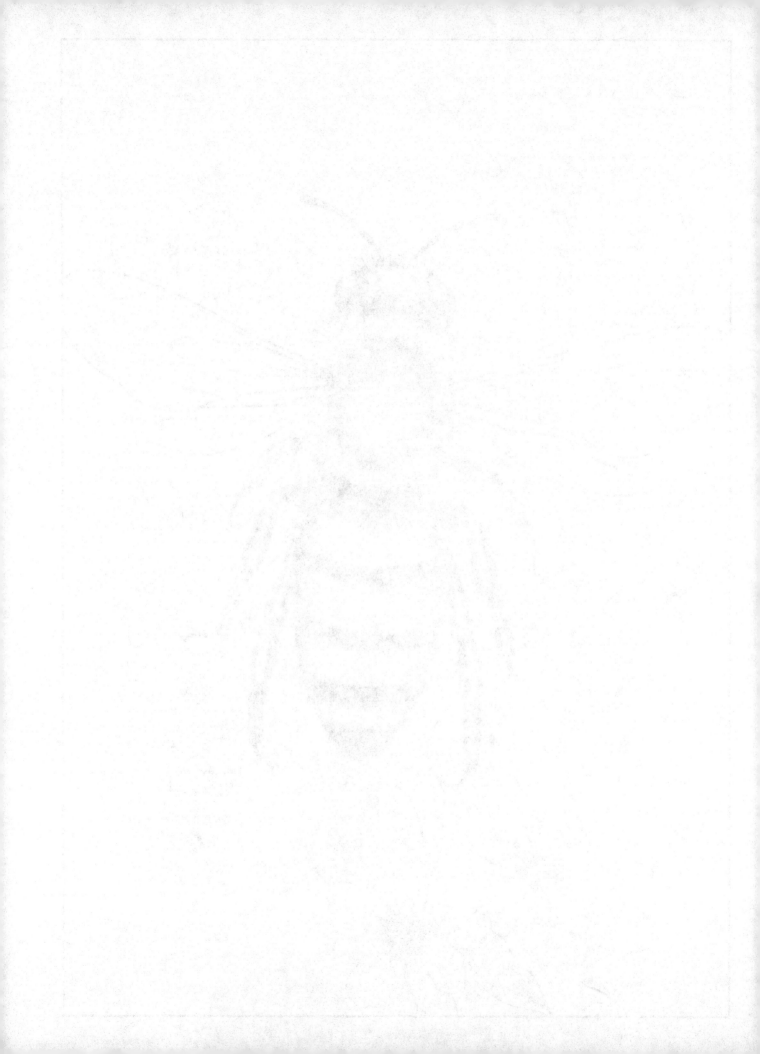

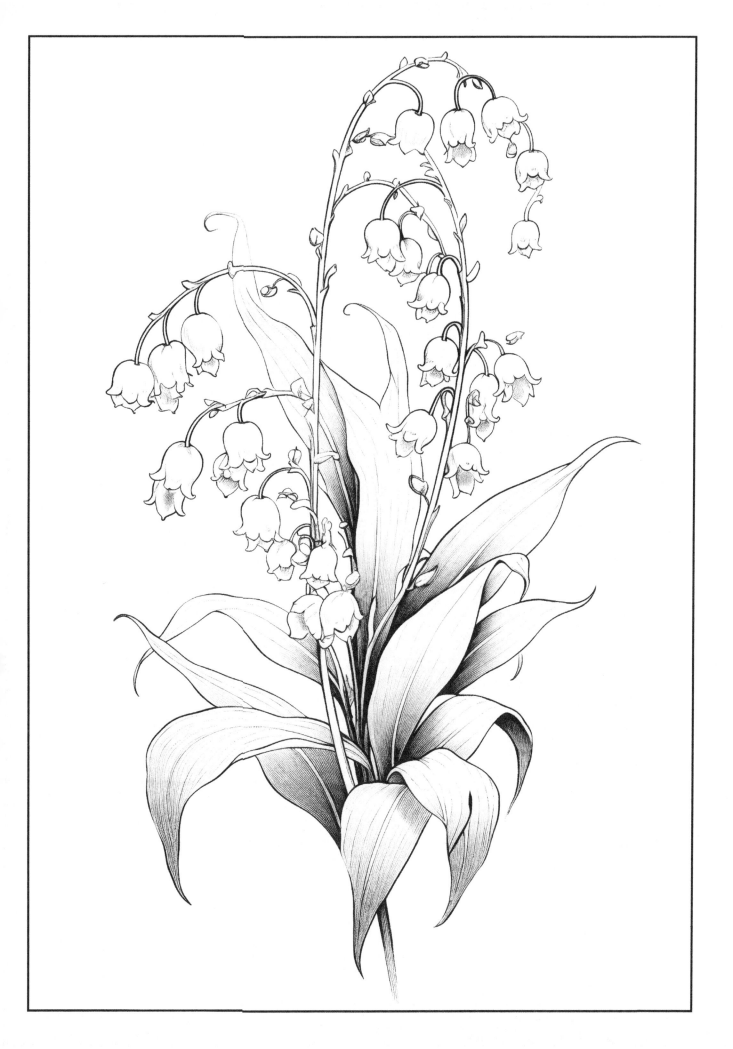

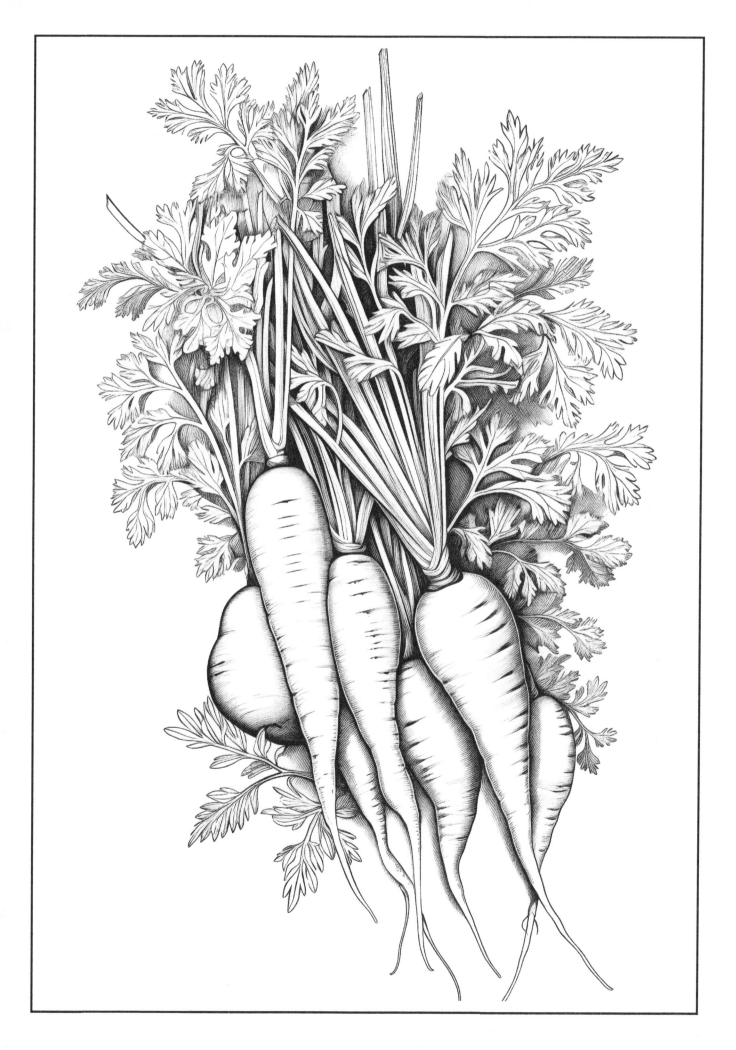

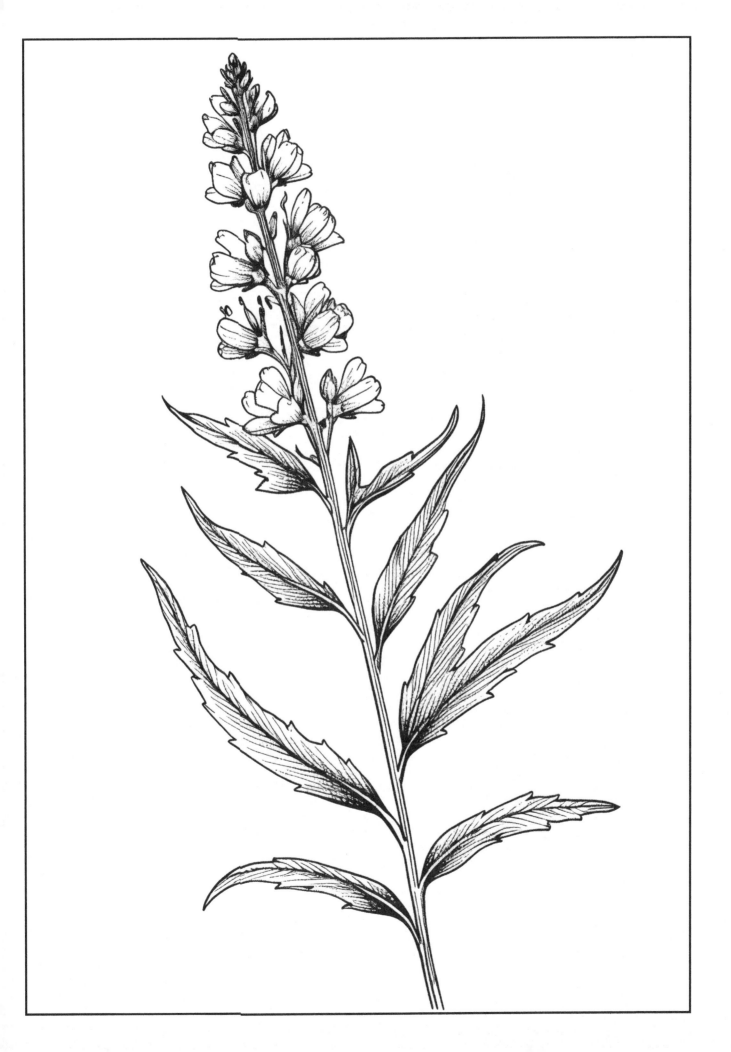

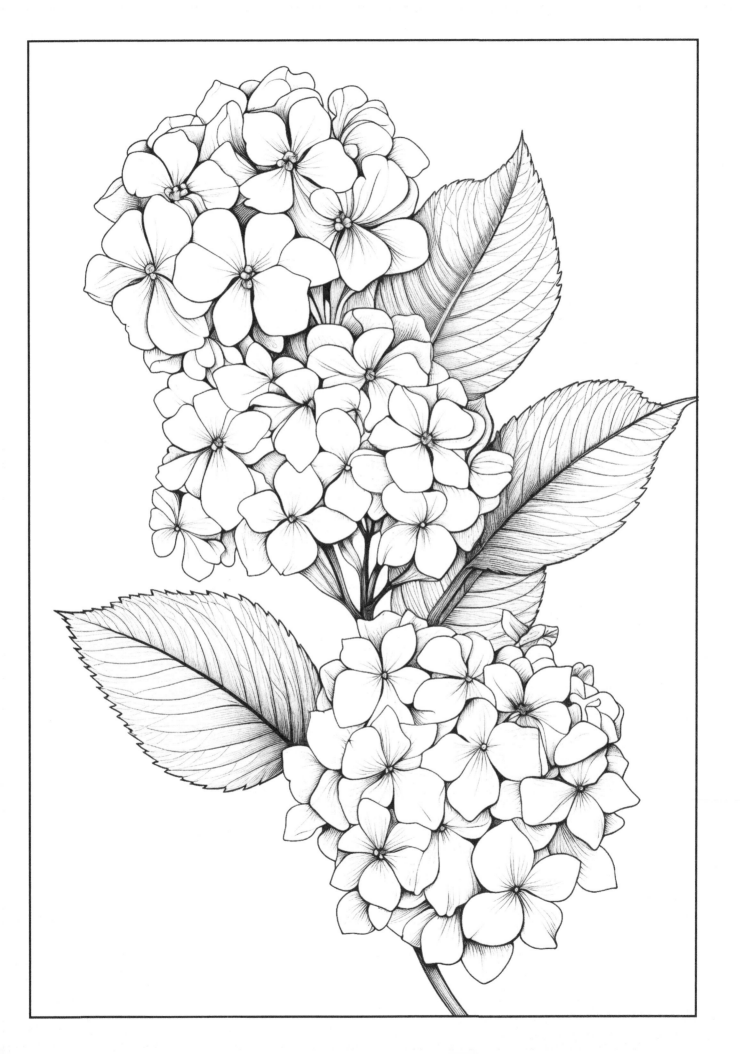

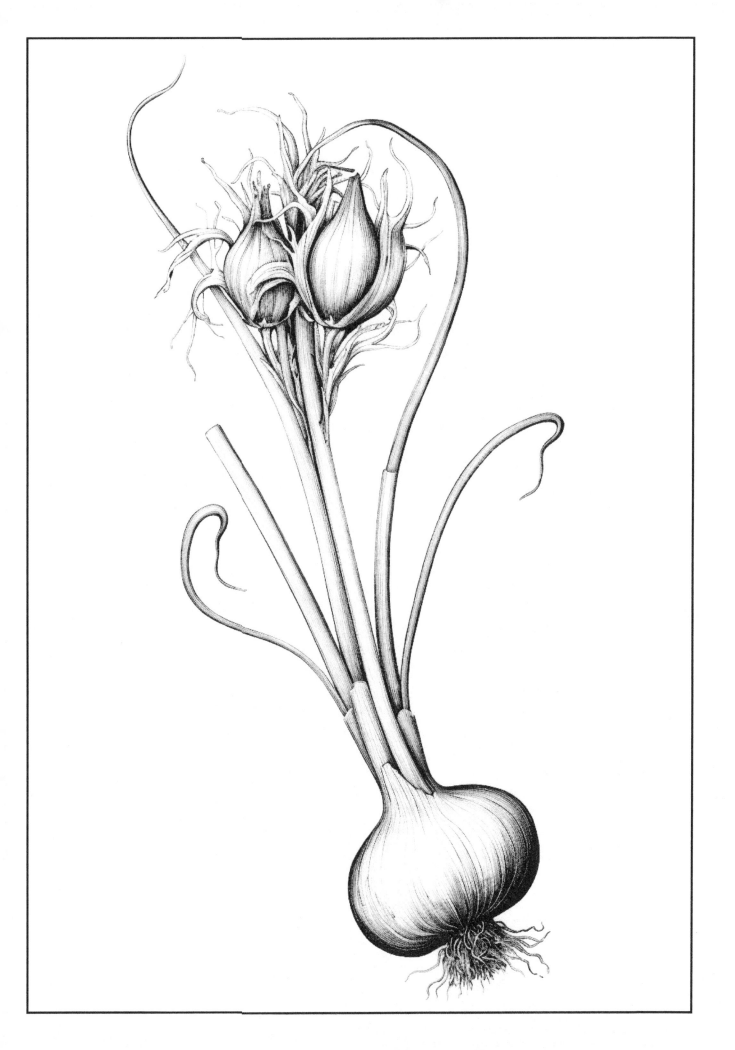

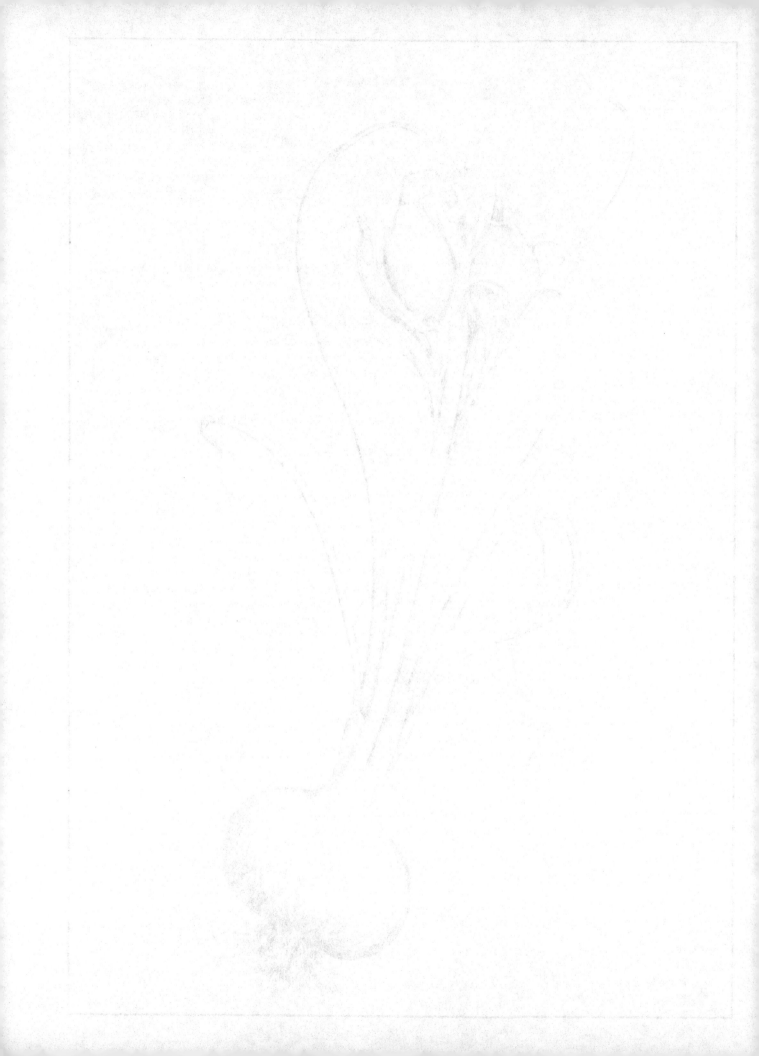

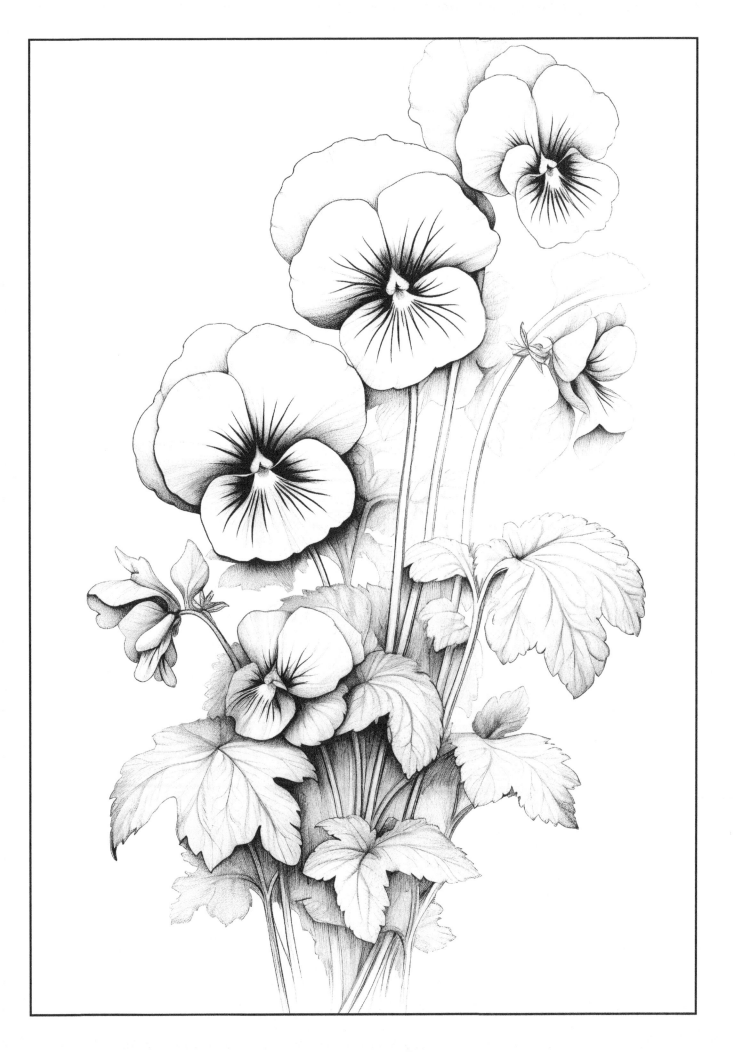

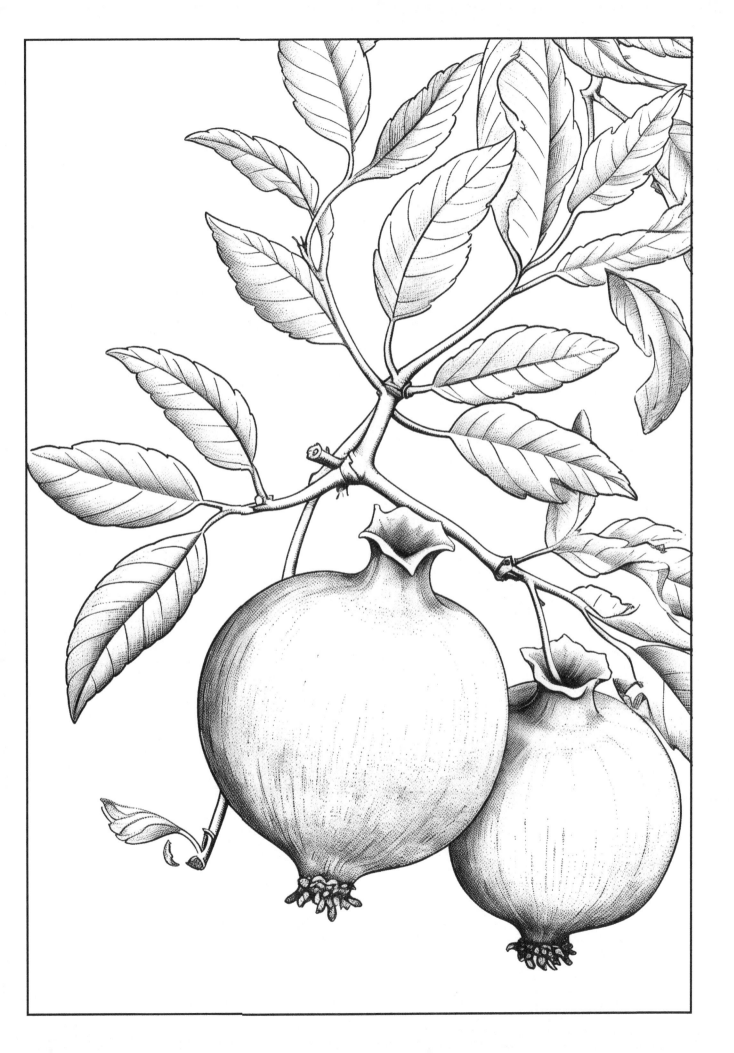

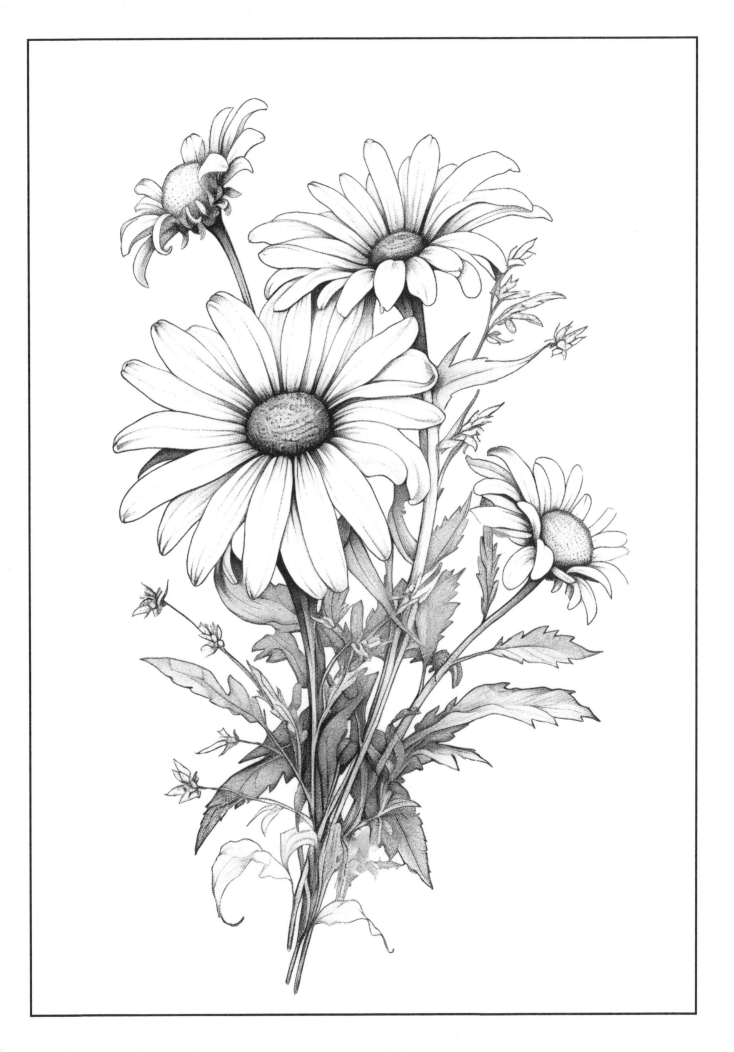

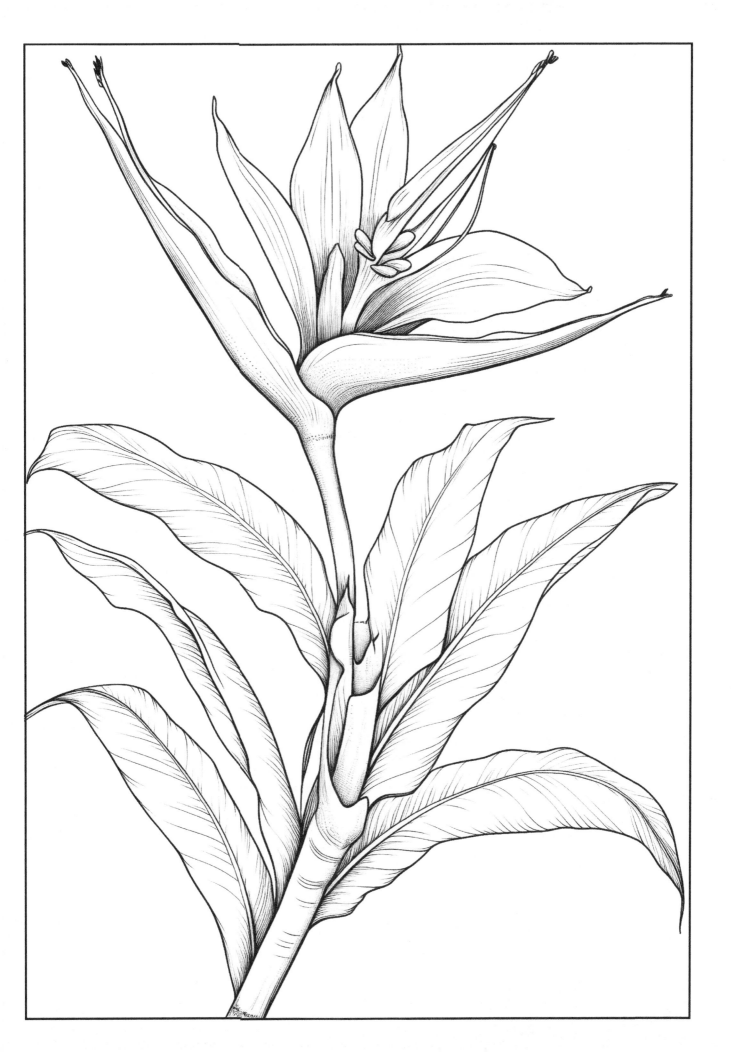

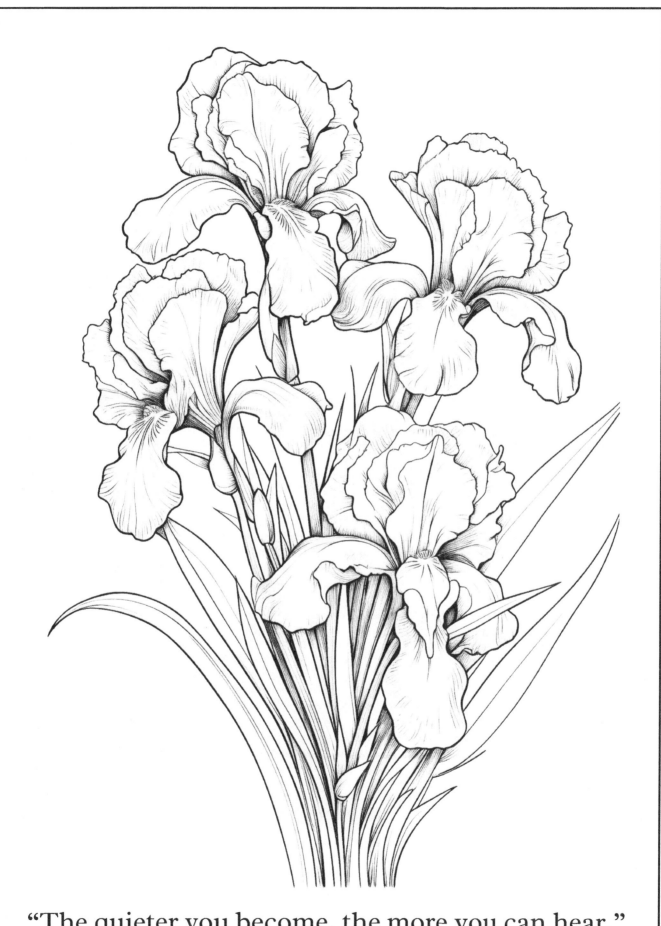

"The quieter you become, the more you can hear."
— Ram Dass